THANKFUL BLESSED INDIVIDUAL

NEVER STOP BELIEVING IN MIRACLES

RYAN YOUNG
WITH LEO WARD

Thankful Blessed Individual

Never Stop Believing in Miracles

Ryan Young with Leo Ward

Copyright © 2018 by Ryan Young

Five Stones Publishing, a division of

The International Localization Network.

Non Fiction

International Localization Network

RandyJohnson@ilncenter.com

Ordering Information:

Special discounts are available on quantity purchases by corporations, associations, and others. For details, contact the publisher at the address above.

Printed in the United States of America

Foreward

I first met Ryan Young in September of 2017 just over a year ago at a staff meeting at People Inc. He gave a talk that day that was very inspirational and it truly moved me at a very deep level. His talk that day about his exceptional life and what someone with a Traumatic Brain Injury could accomplish had the room full of people who work with those with special needs fully engaged in each word he shared.

Ryan is an example of what can happen when someone, can do with their life when they focus on what you can do and not what you can't, a message that applied to each of us. Ryan's optimism and clarity of thought and moral fabric shone through his talk and more importantly his life that day.

Traumatic Brain Injury has left a mark on Ryan, you can tell, it takes a second more time for Ryan to respond sometimes. However, when Ryan does respond, he does so with clarity, kindness, and sensitivity.

Ryan credits his mom, his friends, his support team from People Inc., but most importantly Ryan gives God the full credit for his most amazing life. Each day Ryan demonstrates what can happen when someone's heart has been given to the Lord. Enjoy this book as Ryan shares that heart with you.

Randy Johnson

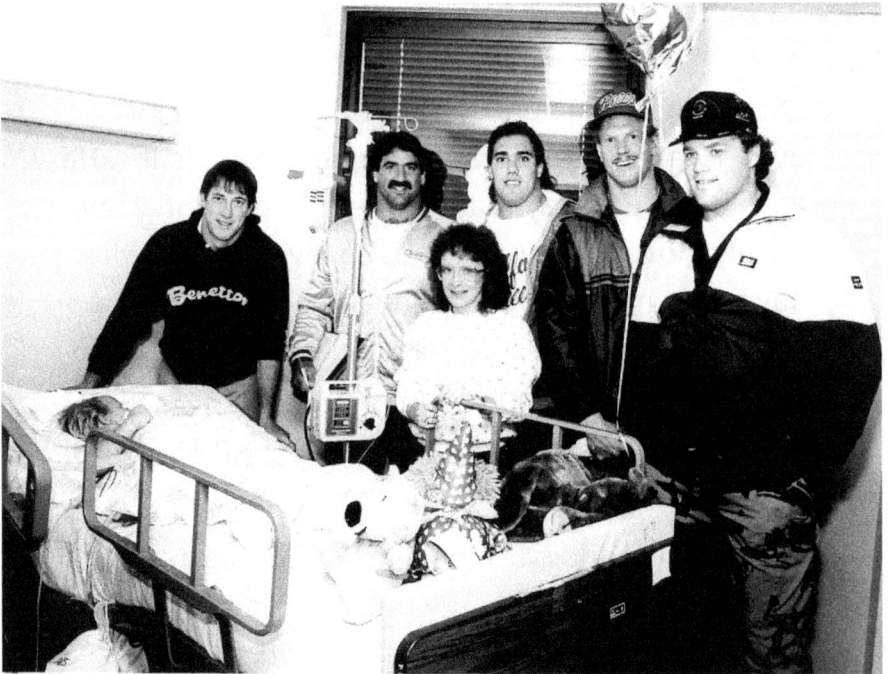

Bills football players came to see me - including Jim Kelly, Fred Smerlas, Shane Conlan, Pete Metzelaars, Sean McNanie and my mom, Jim Kelly who placed his hand on my left shoulder while I was in my hospital bed. My mom was there in the middle. My mother had the picture put in the Buffalo News. The picture below is of me ready to go home.

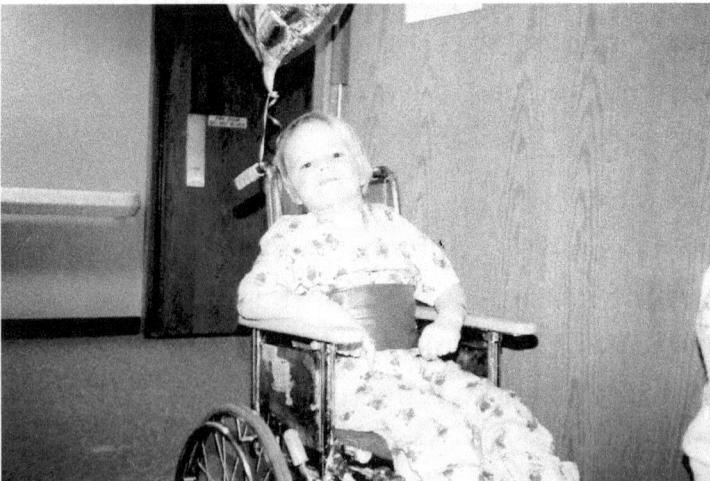

Chapter 1

The Beginning

When I was four years old, my mother and father separated. My mom, my brother Steven and I moved back to Gowanda, New York, where my mother was from. All of my life has been lived in various places in Western New York. We lived with my grandparents. It was while we were living there that I first saw a photograph of my grandfather when he was in the Army.

I don't remember every detail, but he looked good in his uniform someday, I wanted to look just like that. That was the first time I thought about becoming a soldier, but those dreams would be changed forever when I was five years old. My mother found an apartment across the street from her best friend Patti and her son Jim. We moved there.

Dreams changed ...

It was Labor Day weekend,1987. I was five years old. My brother Steve's friend Jim, who lived across the street, came over to see if Steve could come out and play. Steve was grounded for something or other. I asked him if I could play with him instead.

While we were playing outside Jim said he had to go back home for something. I asked him if I could go with him and he said, "No ... I'll be right back." I felt kind of sad and wondered if he really would be right back even though he said he would.

He began walking toward his bicycle and I asked him again if I could go with him and he gave me the same answer. I thought, "Is he done playing with me now? Is he just saying he'll be right back?" When he had gotten on his bike and was about to pedal away, I asked him if I could go with him, for the third time and this time he said, "Okay," and I began to follow after him.

He was riding his bike so he was already on the other side of the street by the time I reached the curb at the end of the sidewalk. I felt comfortable believing now that he really did want to continue playing with me. Before crossing, I looked both ways and saw that there were no cars coming, so I began to cross.

Drunk driver ...

I couldn't see the car driven by a drunk driver speeding down the wrong side of the street right toward me. When he saw me he tried to stop but was too late and he hit me. The impact was so hard that it literally popped me out of my shoes and sent my five-year-old body flying down the street.

The drunk driver that hit me ran to the neighbor's house and pounded on the door screaming, "Call an ambulance! I just hit a kid!"

Many of the neighbors heard the squeal of the tires and ran to see what had happened. My mother's best friend, Patty, ran down the driveway to see what had happened. She said that when she got to me my lips were already turning blue. She began trying to help me breathe. The man that had been driving the car behind the drunk that hit me went up to Patty and told her, "I'm a paramedic, would you like me to help?" She immediately said, "Yes! Please!"

Revived ...

All the details that I am sharing now are things that have been told to me by other people. I have no recollections of my own because I was unconscious and had actually died at the scene. They said that I had stopped breathing. The paramedic gave me mouth to mouth. He brought me back to life.

Our apartment was on the second floor of the house we lived in which was also the house that I was hit in front of. When I was hit by the car my mother was upstairs talking with my grandmother. My neighbor ran upstairs and beat on her door screaming, "One of your kids was just hit by a car!" My mother raced down and were immediately at my side. The paramedic that took over for Patty was giving me mouth to mouth resuscitation at that time and I soon began breathing again, but I entered into a coma that lasted for nine weeks.

I was taken to Tri-County Hospital in Gowanda first. My mother was driven to the hospital by a neighbor and my grandpa came to be with my mom. I was at that hospital for about an hour when the doctor said that I was seriously injured and would be airlifted to Children's Hospital in Buffalo by Mercy Flight. I had suffered a head injury, a broken hip and leg. My mother went to the hospital with my father and a good friend. My brother Steve stayed with my grandma and grandpa, Lucille and Lee.

No good news ...

The doctors were not very encouraging to my parents. They all said that I was going to die. There was little hope and it was just a matter of time. All my mother was able to do was hold her head and cry. "I'm going to lose him! He's going to die! I know I'm going to lose him!" She said.

I was unaware of what was going on around me, but I look back now and can only imagine what a horrible experience this had been for my mom, dad, grandparents ... and for everyone that loved me. My mom was helpless to do anything. All she could do was look at her poor five-year-old, she had been told there was no real hope for ... and cry.

Out of my coma ...

Finally I came out of my coma after nine weeks. The injury to my brain was called Traumatic Brain Injury, or T.B.I. for short. I had an eight hour surgery on my left hip and a cast on my right leg. The doctors all thought that I would never walk again. During my recovery time at the hospital, family, friends and five of the Buffalo Bills came to see me. Fred Smerlas, Shane Conlan, Pete Metzelaars, Sean McNanie all came and Jim Kelly, placed his hand on my left shoulder while I was in my hospital bed. I even had my picture taken with them and my mother had the picture placed in the Buffalo News.

When my parents and friends told me what had happened, I was sad. When they told me of all the help I got, I became very grateful. They told me two big things the doctors said. First, that I was going to die and then they found out I was going to live, but I would never walk again. When I found out I was going to live, I was so very grateful, and will be forever!

Without realizing it, God was working out His plan for my life. His plan was not the same as the doctor's... God gave me a life to live and has been with me ever since.

Changes in my life as a result of T.B.I.

When I came out of my coma, I had to start rebuilding my life all over again. I was an infant in a five year old body. I began speech and physical therapy. I don't have a clear memory of those days, but I do remember they were not easy times. Twelve weeks after I entered Children's Hospital, I was on my way home. God had plans for me ... I lived.

I suffered much worse when I first came out of the hospital. But due to the great physical therapy and physical activities I am now engaged in, things have gotten much better. But I will still be disabled for the rest of my life.

When I started this book, I looked up some of the things one must deal with as a result of such a brain injury. Some were:

- **The Physical Changes** - motor coordination, hearing and visual changes, spasticity and tremors, fatigue and weakness, taste and smell sensitivity, balance, mobility problems, speech impairment and seizures.

- **Cognitive Changes** - memory, decision making, planning, sequencing, judgment, processing speed, organization, self-perception and problem-solving.

- **Behavior Changes** - depression, mood swings, disinhibition (or is a lack of restraint in normal social conventions), impulsiveness, poor risk assessment, poor response to social cues, difficulty in relating to others, low self-esteem, stress, anxiety and frustration.

- **Walking** -- a big challenge I had to overcome ...

I remember on my way home from Children's, that the doctors told my parents that I may never walk again. I had to wait and see how well my hip healed and if it would grow. I truly wanted to walk again. I knew that I would miss so much of life if I couldn't walk. Walking became such an obsession to me. In my heart, I knew I would walk again.

It took a lot of work over the next three years, but I finally was able to walk just fine. Then I began to journey up and down hills on beautiful days and it became an adventure. The doctors said I was going to die and if I lived, that I would never walk again. God had other plans!

I was grateful to be alive for sure, but now I was overwhelmed that I could walk again! God took every step with me then and still does today. It was He that made the adjustments in my balance that I needed to be able to walk. It was God that planted in me the idea that despite what the doctors or anyone else thought, if I tried, I would be able to walk again. That's why I say, that God was with me for every step then and now.

Things do get easier as time goes on, but there are still obstacles one faces every day that most people have no clue of.

Daily challenges with T.B.I. ...
Brain injury survivors are the most extraordinary people on earth under the most horrible circumstances and they become more even more amazing because of it.

Things that a brain injury survivor lives with:
This part of life has not been easy. Feeling a lot of deep hurts, dealing with so much, life feels very frustrating. It seems like no one understands, you do not even understand yourself. You feel broken and not good enough.

Getting angry at someone with an injured brain for being slow, running late or forgetting an important thing, is like getting angry at someone with a broken leg for not running a marathon fast enough.

Recovery after brain injury is a marathon, not a sprint. Go slow and steady if you must, but never give up!

There are a lot of times when it feels like things will never get any better, but then they do. Such is the unexpected life that unfolds for many of us after a brain injury. It is all because of the great loving life God has planned for us.

No one ever apologized for hurting and changing me, but I've apologized millions of times for being hurt and changed by it. I'm trying my best! Not every disability is visible. Brain injury is invisible.

Saying you're fine when going insane. Saying you feel good when you're really in pain. Saying it's nothing when it's really a lot. Saying you're okay when really you're not.

Brain injury survivors should remember this: Before you or anyone else puts you down, please consider everything you have gone through to get to who you are. Every moment you pushed beyond your obstacles & struggles. You are a champion! You are an inspiration to many and you are worthy of nothing less than the deepest unconditional love.

Chapter 2

The Road Back

The day after I was released from the hospital, I began going to school in Springville at the League for the Handicapped. I was able to walk with leg braces and a walker. It was very hard for me to do.

As I grew older I kept having to go to different town schools as special education for students with TBI was still not well established. The state just kept putting me wherever they thought I could fit in. After attending the school in the League for the Handicapped Center in Springville, I went to Eden and North Collins for elementary school. I was very frustrated at that time because I lived in the Gowanda school district, but none of my schools were in Gowanda.

Finally, I was able to go to Gowanda for my middle school. All through my school years, the thing that frustrated me the most was not having any friends. Maybe it was because of my handicap people were afraid to talk to me or whatever, but eating lunch alone was not very fun and walking down the hallway with almost no one saying hello to you is not a good feeling.

During that time, my brother Steve was playing football. I knew I couldn't play football because of all the tackling, but I really wanted to play baseball. There is no tackling in baseball. I would daydream ..., "*There I was at the plate; bat in my hand; here comes the pitch and POW! I connect and it's ... gone! Homerun! People are on their feet; my mom is on her feet cheering, so surprised and proud; as I cross home plate, my teammates all pat me on the back and say, 'Nice hit, Ryan!' Every one of them was my friend.*" Even if I wasn't the star of the team like that daydream, I wanted to at least be able to play!

So much for daydreams ...

My mother asked the doctor if I could play baseball and he said, "No. He can't play any contact sports and baseball is considered a contact sport." My mother tried to get me into karate, but when she told the master about my injury and disability, he said, "No." My only sport growing up was bowling. So, I bowled ... but I thought it was boring, because there isn't much exercise in it! Besides bowling, I liked shopping, but I wanted more out of life. I enjoyed going shopping with my mother.

When my mom got the answer from the doctor about baseball and when the master said, "No," that just added anger to my frustration. I wondered, "Am I ever going to do the things that my brother Steve is doing and have a lot of friends like he does?"

No two traumatic brain injuries are alike, just like there are no two people that are alike. Maybe because of all the negative things my mother heard about my injury, I think she believed that my TBI was worse than it really is. She thinks there are a lot of things that I don't know how to do by myself, and that gets me angry. Sometimes when I would show her that I could do something she didn't think I could do, she would say, "I didn't know you could do that! You just taught me something!" Most of the time when she says that, I just say to myself, "Okay, whatever."

I was getting a lot of counseling when I was in school. I still received some after I was through with school, but not anymore.

My mother, Steve and I had moved to Collins to be closer to my grandparents. I usually went to my grandparent's house after school because my mother had to work. My grandma and I would play board games, card games and sometimes shoot pool on a pool table that my grandpa had made. My grandma would tell me stories about my grandpa when he was in WWII. I was so proud of him. She showed me pictures of him in his uniform. I wanted to look just like that someday. That was when I knew I wanted to be in the military. My grandma also used to take me to church with her. I loved spending time with her so much.

Going to my grandparents made me happy. I could feel the love they had for me because of all I did with them. I loved hearing stories of what my grandpa did when he was younger. When I was home, I usually watched Disney or cartoon movies. I felt lonely without many friends. That seems to have been the worst thing that I remembered about my childhood ... loneliness. It was as if no one on earth wanted to be friends with me.

My mother, Steve and I soon moved to Perrysburg. It was still in the Gowanda school district about ten miles from my grandparent's house. While living there I made friends with the family across the street. Sometimes their daughter would take me for a ride on their four-wheeler. They also had a big trampoline and I had a wonderful time jumping up and down on it. Her father loved to play golf and owned his own golf cart. On nice days, he'd let me drive it around the yard. Then he took his cart to the golf course and sometimes took me golfing with him and let me drive the cart for him. I had a wonderful time living in Perrysburg.

As I said, all of my kid years, I was very unhappy. I was so unhappy I felt like killing myself most of the time. I never actually tried to commit suicide, but I had thought about it. I couldn't understand that I could have changed so much because of a bump on the head. There seemed to be two of me in one body now — the old me and the new me. At times, it was hard trying to live up to the expectations of either of us. Between my TBI and the way my mom treated me by saying things like, "If you want to be treated like a grown-up, stop acting like a baby!" It was hard to know how to act like a grown-up. She was always treating me like a baby, I couldn't do all the things my brother was doing. I also think one of the reasons I was so unhappy at that time was because I didn't have a dad. My mom didn't find her boyfriend, Rick, until I was in my mid-teens.

I would often be called names because I was not as quick to respond as others. I would eat slower than others and people would make remarks that were hurtful. It would make me frustrated and feel sad. Sometimes it would make me cry. I cried often when I was young. People can be very hurtful. I may have been slow to do things, but I was never slow my feeling things.

When I was between ten and twelve years of age, that unhappiness resulted in me throwing a punch at my mother one day. She thought I was going to fight her, so she called my brother to help and defend her. I think she was just calling him to come and stop a fight from happening, but he carried it further than that. The next morning while I was waiting for the school bus, he hit me on the forehead with a baseball bat. I went back into the house and my mother took me to Tri-County hospital where they had to stitch up my head.

During those middle years, I went to the Gowanda school system. After school, I sometimes stayed late and lifted weights. Between the fun with the family across the street and lifting weights, I was having a good time living in Perrysburg. One sunny day, I walked from my house in Perrysburg, through Gowanda to my grandparent's house in Collins - an 11 mile walk. When I got there, my grandma, knowing my mother would be worried, called my mother and she came to get me when she found out where I was.

I wanted more out of life, and four years after elementary school was over, I competed in the Special Olympics for the Disabled. My favorite subjects in school were math and gym.

As usual, I had trouble making friends with any of the kids at the different schools because most of them didn't live in Gowanda. My mother kept making new boyfriends, it was easy for her because she was and is pretty, but once she got to know them and how difficult they were to get along with she broke up with them and continued looking for the right one. Then she met a man named Rick who knew a lot about taking care of kids because he had four of his own. At that time, we were living in Dayton. While he is not perfect she sure does seem to love him, and I think some of that is because he was good to me. He knows how to take care of many things. He is a loving father and knows how to show it in many little ways. I think his kids and my mom and me make a real nice family.

The landlord wanted to move back in. Steve and all of Rick's kids had grown up by then and had moved out, but my mother, Rick and I were having trouble finding a new house to move into that was in the Gowanda school district.

My high school years were with BOCES Work Experience for the Disabled in East Aurora (BOCES stands for the Boards of Cooperative Educational Services, to provide shared educational programs and services to school districts within the state). During this time I got experience working. My first year there, I was cleaning dishes at a local school cafeteria.

My second year was in Jubilee's bakery and my third year was at Burger King. The manager at Burger King liked the way I worked so well that he wanted to hire me, but I was still living in Gowanda so he couldn't hire me. I felt great when I found that he wanted to hire me and then really bad when I found out that he couldn't hire me.

I remember being confused and wondering, "Where are we going to move next?"

Before my fourth year in high school, though, I was still in the Ormsby Program, which is part of BOCES. I went into Tops Markets on my own and filled out an application. I was called in for an interview and was hired on my own. It was a regular job with a weekly paycheck while I was still in high school. I was arranging the shopping carts and carrying groceries out for the customers. I loved that job. It may have been because it meant me reaching out for independence and by getting that job on my own, I felt like I could do something for myself. I felt pride then--that's a good feeling.

By the way ...

The drunk driver that hit me and changed my life and the lives of my family members forever received a

$500.00 fine, suspension of his driver's license for one year, and 1,000 hours of community service. This was his second drunk driving offense.

My mother was told by the DA that the judge had a drinking problem of his own and was usually lenient toward drunk driving offenses. The DMV refused to give him his license back even after several years.

It took my mother seven years to get the case closed. Meanwhile, I kept going to physical therapy, occupational therapy and speech therapy to try and put the pieces of my life back together.

Chapter 3

On The Move

At that time, Rick's parents who had lived in Amherst, NY passed away. Rick, my mother and I moved into Rick's parent's old house in Amherst. I was about 19-years-old then and stayed in Amherst about one month.

I wasn't done with school yet. My mother had been talking with People Inc., a non-profit agency that works with people with special needs. They didn't have a group home near us at the time, but had a place for me in East Aurora. There were eight other people living there. I said, "Okay, I'll move to East Aurora, finish school and maybe find a job." I lived there for about a year. The only things I liked about living in East Aurora was my job at Tops and some of the staff.

Duplex in Amherst ...

The staff personnel where I was living were very helpful and thought I didn't need a lot of help, so they found a duplex group home for me in Amherst with five other people living there. Everyone there had their own room and it wasn't a 24-hour staffed group home. I stopped my job at Tops and moved back to Amherst. Once I moved back there I started buying comedy and action movies. My growing collections of DVDs made having to quit my job at Tops easier. One of my favorite comedy stars was Jim Carrey and my favorite action star was Chuck Norris.

I didn't like my roommate at East Aurora plus there were a lot of restrictions that I didn't need. I stayed there for my last year in high school and then moved to a place in Amherst called Glen Haven. I had to quit my job at Tops, but at least the home I moved to was not 24/7 supervision. The manager only came around during the day.

I was happy when we moved to Amherst because there was a lot more to do there. I was not happy with the first bedroom they gave me because it was the smallest room there and there wasn't really any room to do anything.

The house I lived in was a duplex. Some people with greater needs were on one side and those with lesser needs were on the other. At first, I was in a very small room on the side that needed more help. After 4 months, I was moved to the other side because the manager traded rooms with one of the roommates that needed more help than I did. My new roommates were Nathan and Jeff. Jeff told me how to get to the Galleria Mall by bus.

I lived there for 14 years before moving into my own apartment.

Helping others ...

Sue Martin, one of the staff members, was sad about losing her husband who had recently passed away. I told her how sad I was growing up with an injury and how I was disabled, and most of all, how I had no friends. After some days of hearing about how sad she was, it actually helped me to begin living more positively, that also helped her get over her sadness.

I was amazed to find out that someone else was very sad. It helped me to know I wasn't the only one that felt that way. We were helping each other during that time. We would talk and sometimes go to lunch together. I think that God used the fact that I lost some things to put me in a position to help other people with their losses.

The Bible says in 2 Corinthians 1:4, *"He (God) comforts us in all our troubles so that we can comfort others. When they are troubled, we will be able to give them the same comfort God has given us."* That's what I think happened with Sue and me.

After I was able to help Susan Martin with her feelings, her daughter told her about a dating website. She went on it and found a new husband! She never thought she could be happy again, but God had His own plan for her life just like He did for me … and probably you!

I'm happy that I've been able to help other people several times in my life. Once, on my way back from a concert, I helped a man that had just lost his girlfriend. I said, "Everyone enters our life for a reason. Some come and go so quickly, and some stay for a couple of weeks, months, years and then they leave. The ones that stay for a lifetime are your true friends. Everyone comes for a great reason and that's part of the way God is giving us his strength— getting us prepared for our future.

New adventures …
Sometimes Sue would tell me to get a job. I usually just kept quiet, but other times I would tell her that I know other people that don't have jobs. Then she would say, "Yes, but they're doing something." I'd say, "I'm doing something."

In June of 2008, Nathan and Jeff moved out and Jeremy moved in. He was riding the NFTA, which is a bus and rail system, around for a while. He and I became very close friends and he also told me a way to get to the Galleria Mall by NFTA. One day I decided to try it and kept doing it for several days. I slowly got used to the NFTA system and began taking it to other places as well. I was riding all over Erie and Niagara Counties. I was a little nervous, but my heart was telling me, "Go try it!"

I found a job at a Target Store in Cheektowaga, organizing shopping carts and carrying packages for the customers to their cars.

One day I asked a girl I was having my 15-minute break with if she would be my girlfriend and she said, "Okay." When she said that, I felt then my heart grow stronger. When my job there ended, I moved away, I felt that I lost that strength. That job had lasted for one year. I finally got tired of the NFTA two hour bus ride each way and transferred to Target on Niagara Falls Blvd. in Amherst.

Social consequences due to TBI ...

I worked at the store on Niagara Falls Blvd. for two years and then was fired because of a mistake I made due to my TBI acting up and affecting my impulses control. I touched a female employee's rear end, which I know was more than inappropriate. She told the manager that if I wasn't fired, she would sue the store. So I was fired. A couple of weeks after I got fired I went back to the store to apologize to her, but she wasn't there. I still regret having done that, but all I can do now is make sure I never repeat that mistake again -- which I haven't.

There were other times my TBI acted up. When I was collecting cans and bottles from outdoors for extra money, I once walked into a Target Store (not the one I worked at). I walked behind one of the cash registers that wasn't being used. I'm not sure what I was doing. I looked up and saw a worker looking at me so, I just took some bags and left.

Sometimes, when I'm out walking I don't pay attention to the road. Luckily for me, the cars have seen me and stopped. There is a road that doesn't have any sidewalk or shoulder. I walk it sometimes because there are not many cars on it. In the summer of 2017 when I was walking on it and not paying attention, a school bus and 2 cars behind it slammed on their brakes because of me. I was very lucky, as I think about it. I say, "God was with me."

There are also times when I lose my balance. Sometimes I catch myself and sometimes I fall. I know that stuff happens to everyone, but to me, I think it happens more often.

It is frustrating when sometimes I say things that don't come out the way I intend and sometimes I am not understood. Sometimes that gets me in trouble and I lose friends. One time I was at the gym and I was talking to one of my friends and we were talking about the movie *Die Hard.* I repeated a line in the movie where the word N***er was used. I lost a friend that day because I used that word. I did not mean to hurt him I don't have any bad feelings about any kind of people. I think sometimes my TBI makes it harder for me to understand what makes people upset.

Sometimes when people talk to me they treat me like a child. This happens with people including staff. This can happen with taking my medication at the right time. The medication said I needed to take it every 6 hours. I didn't want to get up in the middle of the night so I waited until I woke up in the morning. My support staff was treating me like a baby and I told them, "This is *my* body and stop treating me like a baby!" It is hard to say what I want when there are so many people thinking that they know what's best for me. To me, sleep was more important than being so perfect about the time. I didn't mind taking it, but I minded being treated and talked to like I was a little child.

I told my Medicaid service coordinator that I almost used my swear words on the ladies. If Sue Martin, my house manager, hadn't taken me away from the situation and talked to me respectfully I would have used many swear words on them. Just because you are a nurse or even a doctor you can still speak to people with respect.

Two weeks after that, a nurse came back and asked me, "Who's the boss?" My answer was, "God." She laughed a little and then said, "God wants you to do what the doctor says." I kept quiet, or I would have said, "If you think that's what God wants me to do, then I would be dead because the doctor said I was going to die when I was five!"

When I watch police shows on TV, the cops always ask the bad guys they're dealing with the questions quickly and don't give them much time to think. If they ever talk to me, I always need time. I'm slow at thinking because of my TBI.

I have been mugged, I have been treated like I am a child, I have been restricted from participating in sports, and went for long periods of time with no friends at all. These things have hurt me very much. There is something that hurts even more, though it's not something that is talked about a lot, but it's something that keeps happening even today. When I speak and tell someone something, especially people that are supposed to help me and protect me, they don't believe me.

So much more happens inside you than outside you. The most expensive thing in the world can't be bought with money, it has to be felt on the inside...and that is love. Believing someone is a way of showing love. The one that loves me the most sometimes doesn't believe me, and that person is my mother. That is very hard for me.

Back to loneliness ...

After that job ended, I went back to riding the NFTA over Erie and Niagara Counties.

I was so happy when I had a job. I was slowly making friends and then, after two years, it ended. That made me sad. I was back to not having any friends again.

At first, they wouldn't let me use the electronic pusher. I took the written driving test and passed. I had gotten lessons from Steven's Driving School for about three months. After that, I took the driving test and failed the first time, but passed the second time. Then they let me use the electronic cart pusher for the rest of the time I worked there.

My mom let me drive her car with her once, but I messed up -- I almost ran a red light. A year later I went to my dads for something, his house is on top of a hill. When we left to go get something and got to the road, he let me do the driving in his car with him in it. I was doing okay. He said he had to go back to his house for something. I drove into his driveway and he drove the rest of the way up to the house.

Then we went back so I could do another drive. This time he thought I was doing okay. I made it from his house to the road, but I felt nervous because I was not yet fully used to driving. I remember that the driveway was down a hill. I slowly made it down, but I didn't stay totally on his driveway. I broke a little wooden fence and got on the grass.

I messed up again and this time I hit something. It wasn't a serious accident, but now my mom doesn't want to believe that I have my driver's license!

Robbed ...

One time when I was waiting at a bus stop at one of the Metro Rail Stations, a man came up to me and asked for some money to ride the bus. I wanted to be a nice guy and help him out, but once I opened my wallet, the man reached in and took all of my money and left. Luckily I had a bus pass to get home.

Another time, when I was waiting at another bus stop downtown, a man came up to me and said, "Would you like to go see some girls for $40.00?" I said, "Okay." So we went to the house of one of the man's friends. The man had me sit down and started smoking what I thought was just a cigarette. My mother smoked cigarettes when I was a kid, so I didn't think anything of it. But he kept trying to blow smoke in my face, which I didn't like at all. I later found out from a friend that it was dope and that he was trying to get me drugged up. I tried to turn that man into the police the next day, but they said that they couldn't do anything about it.

After that my mom said, "I don't want you to ever go downtown again!" and Rick added, "And don't go to Riverside either!" I said, "Then let me get a car!" They both got quiet about it after that.

Getting in shape ...
One day I was feeling kind of sad after I got home from a bus ride, I laid on my back on the ground and looked up to God and asked Him, "What should I do now, Lord?" I felt Him answering me in my heart. He was telling me to go and join Bally Total Fitness and do some exercises. So, that's what I did.

I learned that Romans 8:28 is true. It says, "... *all things work together for good for those who love God, to those who are called according to his purpose.*" Soon I began seeing how I was called for a purpose by God to help and encourage others. If it wasn't for the bad things that had happened to me, I would not have been put on the path that God had for me to go on. Once you realize you deserve a bright future, letting go of your dark past is the best choice you can ever make.

For the first couple of weeks, I was trained on how to use the equipment they had. I kept going because I enjoyed all the fitness equipment they had. In a short time, I started making friends there. After some months, I started going to Tim Horton's with some friends and sometimes I would meet them at one of their houses or a restaurant for dinner. I was even invited to Christmas parties every year at one of their homes.

I started doing walks and bike rides outside. My longest walk was 32 miles and my longest bike ride was 100 miles. My mom asked me, "Why don't you wear your bike helmet? You got hit in the head when you were a kid, didn't that teach you something? And besides, it's the law!" I said, "It's the law until you're 21 years old and I'm older than that, so it's my decision if I wear one or not!"

My mother asked me once, "Why do you drink soda, it's bad for you. Why don't you drink beer like the rest of the family does?" she was joking but I didn't know that and I told her, "That is what caused the guy to hit me when I was five and started all of my problems in the first place!"

My mom and Rick had a family get together at their house and after the party, neither of them would give me a ride back home because they said they had too much to drink and I'd have to stay there for the night. I looked at my brother and he said,

"Don't be looking at me!" I thought, "I'm not staying here tonight." I got up and walked five miles home because I didn't want to stay there that night.

Beginning of Tae-Kwon-Do ...

One cold cloudy winter day in January 2008, when I was twenty-five years old, I walked into Master Gorienol's Tae Kwon Do school. I wasn't really sure what that was. The master came over and asked me, "Did you ever take Tae Kwon Do anywhere?" I said, "No." Then he asked me, "Why do you want to learn Tae Kwon Do?" I said,"I want to be ready to defend myself."

I joined the schools trial program. After the first week of Tae-Kwon-Do, I got my first award for outstanding achievement and it was then I told the master about my injury and disability. The next day, the master asked me if it was alright to tell the class about my injury and disability. I said, "Okay." So he told the rest of the class.

I kept going because I was enjoying it so much. At the end of January, I earned my *white belt*. In a short time, I started making friends there. At the end of February, I earned my *yellow stripe belt* and the master took me out for pizza. At the end of March, I earned my *yellow belt* and in June I earned my *green stripe belt*.

I felt proud of myself that I found a great Tae Kwon Do school with a great master and a great Tae Kwon Do family.

In July they all sang Happy Birthday to me on my birthday. I kept making more and more friends at the gym and Tae Kwon Do and began doing things with them outside the gym as well. In September, I earned my *green belt* and was the Student of the Month. I was also the Student of the Month for November. In December I earned my *blue stripe belt*. In January 2009, I was nominated into the Black Belt Club and in March, I earned my *blue belt*.

In addition to my regular lessons and workouts, I did 12 tournaments every year, some of which were out of state. I went to seminars taught by masters from other schools and attended a banquet every year.

Tae Kwon Do became such a positive part of my life. I felt great that I found friends who wanted to do things with me outside and could see how far I was coming in Tae Kwon Do. I began to feel like a complete person. I was physically getting stronger and had developed friendships with people that I had a common interest with. They liked me for *me*, not because they had to or were being paid to be around me.

Chapter 4

Growing Up

Strength is not what you can do, it's overcoming the things you thought you couldn't.

Jim, a friend of mine at Bally Total Fitness, asked me, "Would like to do some jogging with me?" I was really happy that someone wanted to do something with me outside of where we usually were with each other. It was like I could really feel his love for me as a person and I immediately said, "Yes. I'd love to." Jim and I began jogging a little at Bally's. Then we began jogging some miles outside. After a few months, Jim asked me, "Would you like to try a city-run?" Without hesitation I said yes. The first city-run Jim and I did together was the 5k Corporate Challenge in 2009. I knew that I'd found a friend that would help me discover some other things I didn't think I could do.

One year when my running partner, Jim, came to get me to run the 8k Turkey Trot with him, he brought his grandniece with him to run with us. At the end of the race, his grandniece was crying a little and said, "It would have been nice if we got an award." I told her, "The big reward is in your heart. Thank God for letting you do this.

Romans 8:28 in the Bible says that "*... all things work together for good to those who love God and are called according to his purpose*". I believe that verse is for me. I can look back on all those bad things that happened to me and I could feel upset. But I can still take time to think how God somehow used it for my good.

You are always a winner if you keep trying and don't give up ...

I knew that it was God's love that let me survive my being hit by that car and so that's why I say "The big award is in your heart. Thank God for letting you do this because there are a lot of people that would love to do it but can't.

In 2013, when we were at Chautauqua Lake, a friend took me to watch her son's softball game. At the end of the game, her son began crying because his team lost. I told him, "Even though your team lost, just keep practicing and don't give up. Then you will always be a winner--no matter what the scoreboard says.

Kayak lessons ...

Almost every summer since I was 8-years-old, my mother and I would go to Chautauqua Lake for a week. When it was getting close to that time in 2009 I told my mom, "I don't want to go down there and just look at some water for a whole week anymore." So my mom looked for some places for me to take kayak lessons. She found a place in Tonawanda, NY.

The next summer my mom and I went to the place where I was taking kayak lessons and she bought me a kayak to take with me to Chautauqua Lake.

In June, I earned my *red stripe belt* in Tae-Kwon-Do.

Everyone at Tae-Kwon-Do sang *Happy Birthday* to me for my birthday and in September, I earned my Red Belt. I was *Student of the Month* for November. My *black stripe belt* was earned in December and in January 2010, I was nominated into the *Masters Club,* and in March, I earned my BoJoDi I belt.

On nice spring and summer days, I took lessons on how to use a kayak from the place my mom found in Tonawanda. I loved being in the kayak because it gave me a feeling of being in control I was completely independent when I was paddling along.

The summer of 2012 was my first year of having a kayak on Chautauqua Lake and I really loved it. I had a feeling of freedom and adventure. It was the greatest!

My next belt in Tae-Kwon-Do was the *black belt* so I had a lot of stuff to prove to show that I was ready to take a black belt pre-test. These things included: a written test, know all forms with two self-defense forms from each one of them, have a 1.5-minute long musical form, 23 one-step sparring moves, 11 three-step sparring moves, break boards, a private lesson, get a buzz cut, have a character reference and be ready for questions from the head table.

I was nervous. Although I'd been practicing everything, I still had this disability to deal with.

I passed the black belt pre-test, so I had to do four practices with a lot of friendly helpers to get ready for the actual test. While the practices were going on, the girl at the front desk said, "Most people leave when they are still color belts." I told her, "That's their choice."

The black belt test was in September 2010. Rick and my mother took me to my test. My mother kept saying over and over about twelve times, "I don't think you're going to pass." About a week after that, I heard that my master didn't think I was going to pass so soon. God had other plans for me ...I passed!

When I got my first black belt I felt very happy and proud of myself and thankful that God let me remember all of the stuff and become a black belt. I also received Student of the Year in 2009, 2010 and 2012 for my attendence and for my achievements.

One cloudy day when I came home from a bus ride, I found a piece of paper on my door that said there was a party next Sunday at the Amherst Church of the Nazarene and that they would love it if I could come to it. I went to the party at the church on the next Sunday and from then on I kept going to church because I was making friends there and I liked what they talked about because I'm a survivor.

Community Service ...

I was shopping in a store when I saw a small amount of money on the floor. I picked it up and gave it to a girl that I thought had dropped it. She took it and never even said thanks, she just walked away to a different part of the store. After I got back home I thought, "It would have been nice if she would have at least said thank you, but I did that for my love for God and to thank him for letting me survive my injuries when I was five. He let me be able to do this for Him."

I walked a lot, as I said, and would pick cans and bottles off the ground when I saw them and

43

return them to stores for some extra money. I also returned shopping carts to the stores they belonged to when I found them next to the sidewalk where people would often leave them. When a friend of mine saw me doing this, he remarked, "That's really a great community service. You clean things up and return carts to their owners!"

Doing something that was helping the community made me feel really good. I began thinking of other ways I could make a positive difference in the society.

Chapter 5

Finding Purpose

As I did more and more physical activities, I wanted to join the military and then maybe become a police officer afterward, but I couldn't do either one of them because of my injury when I was five. It made me frustrated because I had limitations.

I thought, "Okay I can't become what I would like so I guess I will go out and help the cops in volunteer work and find some ways to serve the country without expecting anything back." I became a neighborhood watchman wherever and whenever I was out of my house.

With regards to getting a job. In our society it seems you are not a whole person if you don't have a job. I believe your not a whole person if you don't have a purpose. There are jobs I would love to have, not for the money, but because it would bring me more purpose and satisfaction. I find that my TBI does not allow me to work full time. It also can be quite embarrasing when I don't act appropriately because

I can't think fast enough. I know I am able to help people without it being a "JOB". That takes the pressure off and makes me a more effective person. It allows me to fulfill a greater part of my God given purpose.

In November, a new roommate moved in. After the first couple of months, he started playing music really loud at night. My friend and I didn't like that. A lot of times I kept telling the staff worker, Sue, about it but she didn't do anything about it because he didn't play it loud when she was around.

I thought she would just take my word for it, but that wasn't enough for her. I kept getting angrier because she wouldn't believe me.

That crushed me because she was my friend but would not believe me. Even people that are kind to me sometimes seem like they don't believe me. That's the kind of thing that hurts me even more than being punched.

One day when I was talking with Sue about something, that roommate came down and the three of us had a little talk. The roommate said, "If you don't like it when I play my music loud, you can call over and ask me to turn it down."

Later that night, he began playing his music really loud again. I thought, "The three of us talked about it earlier today, so I guess I'll call over and ask him to turn it down." Once he got my call, he did turn it down, but then he went outside and broke my window with a snowball! It took People Inc. a week to fix my window and they didn't do anything to the roommate.

When he broke my window I was angry; then I was happy and thankful when they finally fixed my window, but because they didn't do anything to that roommate about it, I grew angry again. It seemed as if no one paid any attention to my situation and either didn't believe me or didn't care.

One night he began playing his music loudly again. I knew that Sue will not listen to me and do something about it so this time I called the police to come over and tell the roommate to turn down his music. The police came and told him to turn it down and he did.

After the police left, the roommate came over to my room to have me talk with his friend on the phone. The roommate's friend screamed at me on the phone, "If you ever do that again, he's going to kill you!" I just said, "Okay," and that was it … I thought.

When the roommate came over to get me and had me come over to talk to his friend my thought was, "Okay, whatever," because I had heard that stuff in the past.

Stopped a robbery ...

One spring morning in 2011 the sun was rising as I started one of my long walks. I passed a Wendy's Restaurant and, looking in, I saw something that seemed suspicious going on. A man was taking money out of the cash register. He looked up when I was in front of Wendy's as if I was going to do something, but I just kept going so the man went back to removing the money.

I thought, "This could be a robbery! I'll just go to another parking lot where he can't see me and give the cops a call." Which is what I did.

Once I had gotten to the parking lot of another restaurant, I called the police. One policeman came to the parking lot where I was and I told him what I saw. He said, "Okay, I'll go see what's going on at Wendy's."

I stayed at the other restaurant while the policeman went over to check what was going on. He thought it was a real robbery and called for backup. Eight more police cars came. They placed the man under arrest and put him in one of the police cars. That car took off with him in the back seat. The other seven police officers came over to me and each one thanked me. I said, "You're welcome." They asked where I was going and I told them, "I was just out for a walk." Then they left and I went back to my walking.

I was so glad that I was able to help, but I felt that I was just doing my job as part of the Neighborhood Watch Program.

There was another time that I helped the police. My mother was surprised and she asked me, "Why are you helping the police? Nobody in our family ever helped the police before." Later Rick said, "You're not a cop ... leave it!" My mom said years later that what she and Rick said was out of worry for me. I said, "You're trying to judge me. Worry or judging, you still said it!"

I said, "Grandpa was in the military and I would love to do that, but I can't because of my injury so I help the police when I am out walking as part of my way of serving our country." That's why I loved being in the Neighborhood Watch Program so much, it gave me an identity as a servant for the community. My heart was always fully in it and the fact that I didn't get paid for it didn't make any difference. I felt it was an honor to serve the community that I loved. It was then that I learned that you mustn't let what you can't do interfere with what you can do.

False smoke alarm ...

One early spring morning in 2012 when the sun was coming up, I was getting ready to go do my morning workout at Bally Total Fitness, one of my roommates set off the smoke alarm. Everyone went right outside except the one that set it off. He finally did come out. He immediately started swearing at another roommate. I was a close friend of the roommate that was being sworn at. I was with the one that was doing the swearing, so I started swearing back at him.

I was angry and thinking, "Okay, what's this person that's swearing going to do now? He broke my window, he tried to scare me by having his friend say that he will kill me, and this agency that is supposed to be helping me, isn't doing anything.

We were standing there swearing at each other when the roommate that was swearing at me came up to me and took hold of my hands. I wasn't sure what was going to happen, so I waited about five seconds and then the roommate that had a hold of me took me down between the sidewalk and the road. He laid me face down and put both arms around my neck. Every time I tried to make a move, the roommate's hold got tighter and tighter around my head. I asked this roommate, "Are you going to let go and let me back up?" He said, "Yes if you promise you won't hit me." I promised and he let go and I got back up. Then the roommate went back inside.

I didn't do anything more, but I was still very angry.

The police finally arrived because the smoke alarm was still going off. My friend and I were trying to tell the police what the roommate did to me that started the whole thing. The police went in and spoke to that roommate and he told the police that he thought I was going to hit him. The police left and the fire chief came and shut off the smoke alarm. Everyone went back in and I got ready to go to the gym.

While I was at the gym doing my morning workout, I was wondering if the agency was going to do anything about this or are they going to not believe me because they weren't there when it happened -- like everything else with that roommate

After I was finished with my two-hour workout, I went back home. The staff people were there and told me, "You have two choices. You can press charges on the roommate or you can just let it go." I told them, "No. You're wrong. I have another choice. I can sue him ... but I won't." They were quiet for a minute and then I said, "Okay, I will press charges on him."

I was angry because they left out the third choice. I thought they weren't really looking out for me if they left that third option out. The main reason I want to press charges against him was because of all the other stuff he'd done.

One of the staff took me to the police station. I went to a table with a police officer. I tried to tell the officer the whole story of why I was pressing charges, but once I started saying the swear words, the officer said, "Okay, get up and leave." So I got up and as I headed toward the door I said the end of the story, which is the main reason I was pressing charges.

I was really angry because the policeman wouldn't let me tell the whole story. To me, it looked like the police didn't want to do their job.

The officer asked, "Do you have any more to say about him?" I said, "Yes, he also broke my window and one time when I called you to come down to complain, as soon as you left, he had me talk to his friend and his friend told me that if I ever did that again, he was going to kill me."

I was still angry as I finished pressing charges against him and went back home. The police knew that the place where I lived was a People Inc. house, so they gave People Inc. a call the next day and asked, "Why did Ryan start swearing at the officer that he was talking to yesterday when he was pressing charges on his roommate?"

People Inc. told them, "He wasn't swearing at the officer, he was trying to tell him about what had gone on yesterday morning. It all started with swear words." The policeman told that to the officer and the officer said, "In that case, I'm sorry for making him get up and leave without saying all of it. I just didn't understand exactly what was going on."

The People Inc. worker told me that the officer was sorry. I asked, "Which one, the one in the morning or the one I spoke to when I was pressing charges?" The People Inc. person just kept quiet. The apology didn't really mean much to me and I was still angry.

Two days later another police officer came to my house and asked, "Do you know where that roommate lives now?" I said, "No." The officer said, "Okay Ryan, you are going to be put on protection from that roommate for one year. If you see him come near you, we will put him in prison for three years." I said, "Okay." and the officer left.

During that year, I did see that roommate and called the police. When they arrived, the roommate was gone. They said, "Do you want us to put him in prison or just talk to him?" I said, "Just go talk to him." The police said, "Okay, but if you see him again it's prison for sure." I said, "Okay," and they left. I didn't see that roommate for the rest of that year.

New gym ...

In February 2012, Bally's Total Fitness closed. My friends and I were all sad because we all had to find a new gym to join. It took some months, but I finally joined LA Fitness and some of my friends also joined. The friends I had from Bally's that didn't joined LA Fitness still go to Tim Horton's together and still get together for a Christmas party every year. Jim and I still do 5k runs with each other.

Chapter 6

Famous? ...

In December of 2012, I took my Second Degree Black
Belt test. After four practices with a lot of friendly
helpers to prepare for it, I passed. Then at the annual
Christmas party that I go to every year, I got the
chance to meet up with a Mr. and Mrs. Jacob who
handles a group of kids in Lockport, NY and a group
of seniors in Olcott, NY. I told them about my injury
and disability and what I do now in life to overcome
it. They asked me, "Would you like to come and give
a speech about your life to our groups sometime?" I
said, "Okay."

It felt great that I passed my second-degree black
belt test. I was thankful for all the friendly help that
I received. Every year I love getting together with
those friends to have a Christmas party. I knew if I
didn't have all this motivational help that my physical
activities have given me, I would be concerned and
nervous, but because all of the inside strength I
gained I could say, "Okay, I can make it." A little part

of my speech is: "Everything that God is having you do now is getting you ready for your future."

In January 2013, I went to their kid's group in Lockport and gave a speech about my life. Some of the kids wanted their picture taken with me and one of them told me, "You're famous." I said, "Thank you. I'm a black belt and one of the roles of being a black belt is showing respect."

It felt so great hearing that from one of the kids … imagine me, famous!

Weathering a real storm …

In the summer of 2013, when my mom and I went to spend a week at Chautauqua Lake I went out in my kayak. It was nice when I went out, but in a while, a rainstorm started. I went over to a boat launch and some nice people there helped me out by giving my mom a call to let her know that I was okay and to come and get me and my kayak

I was so grateful that I found help and I thank God for the two senior citizens that helped me when I got trapped in a rainstorm when I was kayaking. After my mom came and got me. I was really grateful for the fun I had on the lake kayaking and for the help those people gave me during the storm. I thanked them two times for helping me. They smiled and said, "Glad to be able to help you."

One time while I was waiting for the bus, I saw a bunch of kids climbing a fence that was surrounding a tennis court. I thought, "They're doing something dangerous now and they probably won't listen to me," so I called the police and asked them to come and tell the kids to get down because there were no parents around.

I was still waiting for the bus, so I began collecting fallen sticks and making a pile of them between the road and the park. When the policeman was done telling the kids to get down from the fence, he gave me the thumbs up because he knew it was me that called him.

I thought, "Your welcome, officer. Goodbye."

Another speaking engagement and letter of introduction ...

In November of 2013, I received another call from Mr. and Mrs. Jacob. They asked, "Ryan, would you like to come and give your speech to our group of senior citizens in Olcott and have some dinner with us?" I said, "Yes. That would be great."

I thought, "Even though they were thanking me for coming to give my speech, I was still thankful for the dinner."

From then on, I kept going to places like schools, churches and places that worked with people with disabilities and asked them if they would like me to give my speech to them, but mostly only the people that worked with people with disabilities were interested.

I felt somewhat useless because they weren't letting me at most of the schools and churches, but happy when they were letting me in the places with people with disabilities.

I called Mr. and Mrs. Jacob and asked if they could help me in any way to get into places to give my speech. They gave me a paper with two photos. One for when I gave my speech to the kids in Lockport and the other was when I gave my speech to the senior citizens in Olcott. They also gave me a letter of introduction which read:

To Whom It May Concern,
We would like to introduce you to a dynamic young man with whom we had the pleasure of meeting and inviting to speak on two separate occasions. This vibrant young man is Ryan Young. His inspirational talk had a great impact on our groups.

He met with kids in our Alive Junior High Youth Ministry in downtown Lockport. The students listened intently as Ryan shared about the challenges and victories in his life and how he overcame his disabilities to go on and accomplish great things.

When Ryan was 5-years-old he was hit by a drunk driver and suffered a traumatic brain injury. While this caused many years of hardship and difficulty, including bullying from other children as he grew up, Ryan persevered and turn his disability into something positive.

He shared with us how he went on as an adult to find a gym to work out in on a daily basis, challenging himself each day to become stronger. In addition to working out, he walks many miles a day and has a black belt in Tae-Kwon-Do! He shared with us his numerous awards and trophies in the sport. He even showed us his awesome moves and kicks!

Next Ryan challenged a group of senior citizens at a dinner in Olcott inspiring each of them to continue doing what they can do to the best of their ability despite physical limitations. His engaging demeanor and polite and respectful interaction with the crowd endeared us all to him.

Ryan turned his dream of being a military veteran into doing volunteer work in the community. He even shared with us his heroic efforts to save an individual as part of his neighborhood watch activities.

Ryan answered questions from the audience and credited his faith for keeping him grounded, strong and steadfast. We believe Ryan would be an excellent speaker for any age group. His poignant message *and witty sense of humor make him a delight for any crowd. His talk touches on bullying, drunk driving, persevering and following your dreams - basically never giving up! He was such an inspiration to our groups that they all wanted pictures with him and had him sign autographs. It is our pleasure to* highly recommend Ryan Young to come out and inspire your group! You will be forever changed!

That made me feel great and I thanked Mr. and Mrs. Jacob for helping me.

Chapter 7

For a man to have friends he must show himself friendly

As time went on, I kept making more friends. One of my friends, Kristan Plath, that I ran with told me, that her husband, Alan, has a team that's called the Garbage Can Turkeys. They collect money for the Roswell Park Cancer Institute Hospital in Buffalo. His team does the Ride For Roswell every year. She said, "Would you like to join his team and give it a try?" I said, "Yes. That would be great! I'll do it."

I was so happy because I keep finding more friends and that one of them told me about her husbands Ride For Roswell team. I was so uplifted because he let me join his team so I can help people survive because of all the help I got to survive.

Serving my country and community ...

On June 2014, after collecting donations from some of my friends, I did my first Ride For Roswell. Every year since then I've been doing it. because I've been a survivor since I was five-years-old and I was so happy that I found a way to help others survive and a way to serve our country with this activity

One summer afternoon in 2014 when I went to a park to just sit down for a few minutes, I saw a little girl having trouble in a baby swing. I went over to see what was going on and saw that the little girl was trapped in the swing. I tried to lift her out but every time I tried to lift her she said, "Ouch!", so I called the police and told them the situation.

The police transferred the call to the fire department and the fire chief came. That got all the rest of the kids that were playing in the park to come over to see what was happening at the swing. When the fire chief saw that the girl was trapped, he called one of the fire trucks to come with chain cutting pliers to come and cut the chain.

While the chief and all the kids in the park were waiting for the fire truck to arrive, a policeman came and stood next to me and gave me a "thumbs up" for making the call.

When the truck came, the girl's father did also. Once they cut the chain and got the little girl out, the father said, "Thank you." I said, "You're welcome. It's part of my job because my job is being a Neighborhood Watchman. I try to watch out for everyone's safety."

The first week of July I went camping at Sunset Bay with my mom and Patty. I went for a bike ride to Silvercreek. I wasn't expecting to find much there, but I found a People Inc. office there. I walked in, asked them, "Can I give my speech? I'm a disabled survivor." They said, "Okay." I gave my speech there. One of the staff people said, "You should be on TV." I said, "I would like to, but I don't know how." They didn't know how to either, so I left after saying that.

One night in 2015 I was watching the 10 o'clock evening news. I saw that a woman got stabbed in the Walmart parking lot. A few days later when I was coming back from one of my long walks, I found near the entrance to Walmart's parking lot a sharp knife with the blade stuck in the ground.

I went to a part of the parking lot where cars don't usually park and called the police. One policeman came and took the knife from me. I said, "Okay. Bye," but the policeman didn't say anything, he just left. When I got home that day I found a thank you card from the police department on my door.

That made me feel good. Even though I don't do things for thanks, whenever I help someone in any way, to find that thank you letter on my door really made my day.

Whenever people give to others, they also give love...

Later in 2015, I saw on the news that the people from Channel 4 would be going to be at the American Red Cross in August. I thought I would go there and maybe speak with them. So, in August 2015, that's what I did and I did get to speak with the Channel 4 people that day. I also got to talk on the TV News 4 a little about myself. I said, "I give blood because I got hit by a drunk driver when I was 5 and almost died, but a blood transfusion helped me survive.

It felt wonderful being able to talk to Channel 4 people then to be put on TV News 4.

The next week my mother said, "You didn't survive because of a blood transfusion. It was all healing, but that's what you told Channel 4 News." I told my mother, "When people give blood, they are not just giving blood, they are also giving love."

It's like the donations that I collect for the Ride For Roswell. Those people aren't just giving a donation, they are also giving some love. It's love that helped me survive when I was five. Allowing me to do all that I do now in what I do for a living ... which is helping people. I'm thankful for all the love I have received and all the love that I can give.

No matter how good or bad you think your life is at the moment, wake up every day and just be thankful for life. Trust me, somebody somewhere else is fighting to survive as I was doing when I was five years old. That's why I do the Ride for Roswell.

From then on I kept going to the American Red Cross and gave blood often. After several weeks, I told them about my injury. They said, "You can't give blood anymore. But you can volunteer here if you would like to." I said, "I might like to, but I don't have a car. My transportation is the NFTA bus, walk or ride a bike." They said, "Okay, thank you for your giving heart, goodbye." I felt sad for not being able to give any more blood or to volunteer there.

After I was on Channel 4, I was called for jury duty. Just before the trial was to begin, the judge said, "This man is in for drunk driving. Do any of you have a reason that you shouldn't be on this jury?" I stood up and said, "I think I may have a reason. I am disabled with a traumatic brain injury that I got by getting hit by a drunk driver. I give speeches about that now." The judge excused me at that time.

In June of 2017, my service coordinator asked me, "What is your goal?" I said, "I can't join the military so my goal is to be on TV." She said, "You were put on Channel 4 for donating blood isn't that enough?" I said, "Yes I was, but that was only a couple seconds, I want more."

Chapter 8

Doing Good Feels Good

In February 2016, I signed up for the Ride For Roswell and began to collect donations.

In March, I went on one of my long walks but was taking the NFTA bus on the way back. My stop was coming soon and as I stood up, I noticed that someone had left their wallet on the bus. At first, I was a little confused as to what I should do, but then I thought, "What would I do if I was a policeman." I picked up the wallet and got the number of the bus before I got off. When I got home, I opened the wallet and saw an identification card.

I called the police and said, "I found a females wallet in an NFTA bus. I'm home now. Can you come over and get it?" A female officer came over. I gave her the wallet and the officer took my phone number and left.

The officer found where the woman lived that had lost the wallet and took it to her and told her, "A person named Ryan Young found your wallet and turned it in." She also gave her my phone number.

When the officer left, the lady gave me a phone call and asked me if I could meet her the next day at the 7-11 store.

I met her there and she thanked me and gave me $25.00. She said, "There was $525.00 in the wallet and it was all still there." I said, "That's good. I didn't see any of the money. I just opened it and saw your identification card and called the police." She said, "Thank you." I said, "You're welcome. Helping people is part of my job." She said, "You're crazy." Then she smiled at me and left.

One of my friends at LA Fitness gave me the nickname of Crazy Grass Hopper, so I'd just say to myself, "Yes, I'm always crazy!" That's why as part of my volunteer job, I don't want anybody's money.

I thanked her for the $25, but I was thinking that my big payment was surviving the injuries I got when I was 5 and getting through, for all this stuff that I've been able to do and all my friends. Being rich isn't what you have in your bank account, it's what you have in your heart. It always makes me feel good when I'm able to help people.

On June 12, 2016, I took my Third Degree Black Belt test and after four practices, with a lot of great people that helped me get prepared for it, I passed.

I was grateful that God brought me this far and gave me all this help that I needed at different times.

On the third week of June 2016, I was getting ready for the Ride For Roswell. On June 23rd, I saw that my friends had given me enough donations to be put in the Extra Mile Club. That really made me happy and I was really grateful for all the donations that put me in the Extra Mile Club!

A Mixture of emotions ...

In July 2016, I went camping at Sunset Bay for a week with my mom and her friend Patty. At the end of the week, Rick came there to help us pack up and go back to Amherst because my mom and he had a concert to go to. When I saw him I thought, "Okay Rick, let's get packed so you and mom can go to your concert."

I went upstairs to use the bathroom. On my way back down I slipped and fell. I could feel my hand hitting all the stairs behind me, but when I got to the bottom I didn't think it was very bad.

I just felt a slight bit of pain and needed a little rest so I went over to something soft to sit on. My mom said, "Why don't you get up, go outside and help Rick load stuff in the cars?" I said, "I would but my hand hurts."

I wondered, "Does she believe me because she wasn't there and didn't see me when I was falling down the stairs.

My mother began pressing down on all my fingers. When she got to the middle one, I said, "Ow!" Then she knew that I was telling the truth about being in pain. My mother and Rick finished packing the cars and I kept my hand on soft things. After the cars were packed, I got in the car with my mom. Patty said, "Ryan, stay thinking positive." I said, "Okay, I will. Thanks."

I was happy because I knew she did believe me. I was thankful that there were others to finish packing and that Patty told me to stay thinking positive.

When we got back to Amherst, my mom took me to Immediate Care. Rick went to his house to unload the car. The doctor at Immediate Care gave me an x-ray and found that some of my bones were broken in my right hand. He said, "You have to go the Emergency Room at ECMC, (which is the Erie County Medical Center in Buffalo). So my mother took me there. After Rick finished unloading the car he joined us there.

I was happy that my mom took me to Immediate Care instead of going to her house first to unload. I was also thankful that Rick did the unloading. I was sad to hear that I had some broken bones and that

I had to go to Emergency Room at ECMC. I was glad that I had my mom to give me a ride there.

While we were at ECMC, I told my mom, "You and Rick can go to your concert if you want." My mother said, "No, that's okay." We all had to wait six and a half hours to hear from a doctor how to rest my hand. The doctor said, "You're going to need surgery." The doctor told my mom to bring me back in two weeks.

For those six and a half hours I was bored just waiting around, but I was happy because my mom and Rick stayed with me instead of going to the concert. I felt some sadness because I had to take a long vacation from my activities and also sad because I heard that I will have to get surgery in two weeks

From sadness to gladness ...

In two weeks we went back to the hospital. The doctor took another x-ray and said, "You won't need surgery. Your hand is healing very well."

I was so grateful that I didn't need surgery because it was healing very well.

I had been resting my hand for two weeks and then started going back to the gym, but only to ride the bike for an hour. After a week of that, I started going back to Tae-Kwon-Do, but only to help teach classes. It took about three months for my hand to heal.

I was so happy that I was able to do a little workout

A time to be thankful ...

When It was getting close to my birthday, my mother asked me, "What would you like for your birthday?" I told her:

"I already got my birthday presents. They are: all the donations that my friends gave me for the Ride For Roswell to be put in the Extra Mile Club; I passed my Third Degree Black Belt test; I had a great week of camping with you and Patty; you and Rick stayed with me in the ER because of my broken hand instead of going to the concert that you paid $300.00 for the tickets; and after two and a half weeks of not doing much of my physical activities, getting the good news from the doctor that I don't need to go through surgery. Those are all Birthday Gifts to me ... Thank You!"

Independence ...

I thanked God that my hand was doing well and that it only took three months to heal and get back to doing all my activities. In February 2017, I moved out to live on my own.

I was happy that I went back to doing my activities but I was sad because of leaving the people where I lived. Still happy that I was finally able to do most things on my own and be more independent.

How I found my church ...

When I was still living at Glen Haven, there were times when the staff couldn't come get me from Tae-Kwon-Do. So I either got a ride from a friend that did Tae-Kwon-Do with me or I had to wait for the next bus.

On Fridays when I had to wait for the next bus, I usually went for a short walk along Niagara Falls Blvd. I mostly was looking for somewhere to go to keep warm until the bus came. I usually waited for the bus inside a little store called the *Corner Store*. I was passing churches all the time. One was the Christian Fellowship Church and the other was a church that I won't name, but they always had some cars outside.

One night, after my Tae-Kwon-Do, I thought I'd stop into that church and see what was going on, so I did. Kids were in there playing some sport. I stayed and watched the kids play until the bus came. I kept going there every week to watch the kids play until it was time for the bus. One day when I was there someone, either the coach or the pastor, came over to me and said, "You're not allowed to be here, you'll have to leave." So I left. Lucky for me, the worker at the Corner Store would let me stay in the store until it was time to catch the bus.

Two months after I moved into my own apartment I started looking for a new church to join. I thought maybe I'll try going to the Christian Fellowship Church. I went there the following Sunday. They were very friendly to me, so I continued going.

They even gave me rides from my apartment to church and back home again. After the first month, one of the guys that volunteers to be a greeter near the door said to me, "Would you like to hand out the church bulletins? You smile a lot." I said, "Sure, I'll be glad to." So the next Sunday I started handing out the church bulletins. Then I started collecting the church donations and first Sunday of every month I held the bread for communion.

I have been able to give my speech there twice. That's been my church since I moved into my own apartment. I say to myself a lot, "Everything I do, I do it for you, God, to thank you for giving me the two big miracles when I was five and that you don't ever stop showing your love."

Possible head injury prevented ...

In July 2017, on an NFTA bus I was riding, a father
got on with his two daughters. One was bigger
than the other. The father was up front making the
payments when the bigger daughter took a seat
and the smaller one sat down next to her. While the
father was still paying up front, the bigger daughter
decided to change seats. When she did, the smaller
one got up and started running back to sit in the
seat next to her, but when she got up and began to
run to the seat, the bus driver started driving and
the little girl lost her balance and fell backward. I
was sitting right next to where she was falling, so I
stuck out my left arm and caught her before she hit
the floor. The father got through paying and came
back and thanked me for stopping his daughter from
falling on the bus floor.

Enough Tae-Kwon-Do ...

Sometime in 2016, I put on Facebook that I was
getting ready to stop going to Tae-Kwon-Do. At
class that day, the master took me into his office and
asked me, "Why are you getting ready to leave?" I
said, "You know my goal when I started was to be
ready to defend myself. Third Degree Black Belt, ten
years of training is enough. It's not just all you have
taught me, it's also how I had to deal with all these
wars I had in life."

He said, "What kept you here?" I said, "All the friends." He asked, "When will it be ten years?" I said, "The beginning of 2018." My last day of Tae-Kwon-Do was January 17, 2018.

Chapter 9

My Speech

As time went on the speech I gave kept getting longer. It was finally like this:

Hello, I am Ryan Young. The speech I am going to give you is about miracles, drunk driving, bullying, and following your dreams. My advice is to never give up. I turned my disability into something positive. I want to encourage you all to learn and respect yourself and others.

When I was 5, I got hit hard by a drunk driver. The doctors kept saying I was going to die. Family, friends and strangers from all around the world kept praying for me. Then, one night God came down and left something in the hospital for the doctors to save my life. When I got out of the hospital after three long months of being in a coma with a head injury, a broken hip and leg, the doctors said I wasn't ever going to walk again.

Miracles happen every day - you just never know how big they are going to be ...

The only thing it left me with is a traumatic brain injury. During my kid years, I didn't live very well. I didn't have many friends and was very unhappy and bored. I just woke up one day and decided I didn't want to feel like that anymore or ever again, so I changed. I started watching action movies. One of my favorite stars is Chuck Norris.

Before I started all of my physical activities I got mugged twice. The first a man just stole my money. The second tried to get me high by blowing dope at my face. Then one day I was lying in the grass in my backyard and asked God, "What do you want me to do now?"

I could feel Him answering me in my heart telling me to go start fitness in a gym. Because you can't become what you need to be by remaining what you are. Then I started doing long walks, runs and bike rides.

One of my walks brought me into a Tae-Kwon-Do school. Now I have a lot of great friends in the gym, Tae-Kwon-Do and church. There are no limits to what you can accomplish -- only those you place upon yourself.

Physical activities don't just build up body mass, it also helps you mentally and gives you confidence. It helps put more love in your heart and gives you more respect for yourself and others. I know everyone has a different activity they enjoy after school or work, just remember, *he who is not courageous enough to take risks and believe in him/ herself, will accomplish nothing in life.*

There is no exercise better for the heart than reaching down and lifting people up.

That's a great way of showing your love and respect to others. A dream doesn't become reality through magic. It takes sweat, determination and hard work. Strength doesn't come from what you can do, It comes from overcoming what you once thought you couldn't do. If you lose during that activity, just remember you will always be a winner when you keep practicing and do not give up!

Hard work pays off, that's why I strive to better myself on a daily basis. A champion isn't made in a gym. A champion is made from something you have deep inside you -- a desire, a dream and a vision. You have to have the skill and the will. But the will must be stronger than the skill and you have to believe in yourself when no one else will.

Every achiever, I have ever met says my life turned around when I began to believe in myself. We shouldn't be afraid to stand for what we believe in -- even if it means we have to stand alone. Whenever you find yourself doubting how far you have to go, just remember how far you've already come. Remember everything you have faced, all the battles you have won and all the fears you have overcome. Nothing is too hard if you have the courage to try and the faith to believe that anything is possible. That's how I learned that sometimes bad things can lead you to good places in life.

Another thing my physical activities got me into is volunteer jobs. When I'm out walking, my two volunteer jobs are community service and neighborhood watch to help this country be clean and safe. I would have liked to join the military or become a police officer, but I can't because of my disability so I serve and protect the United States of America by doing volunteer work. A soldier doesn't fight because of what's in front of him, he fights because he loves what he left behind!

All of my physical activities are not for hurting people, they are for protecting them. Stop running from people who keep hurting you. Stop wondering why people keep hurting you. Ask yourself, "Why am I continuously allowing this to happen?" Speak up! Stand up for yourself. Sometimes we suffer not because of the violence others inflict on us, but because of our own silence.

It's all part of self-respect and self-defense ...
Who knows, you might not only be defending yourself but others as well that got hurt in the past from the same people. Always remember whatever comes our way, whatever battle we have raging inside ourselves, we always have a choice. It's our choices that make us who we are. We can always choose to do what's right. Sometimes we have to be our own hero and do what's right even if it's a little dangerous. Never let fear be in the way of the ones we love. My biggest ones so far are: reporting a robbery, defending a friend, saving a little girl and turning in a woman's wallet that I found.

If anyone ever asks me if I get paid from any of my volunteer jobs, my answer is, "My payment is surviving when I was a kid, being able to do all that I do and all my great friends that I have."

To be rich is not what you have in your bank account, but what you have in your heart ...

Two more things I do that are for the safety of others, I do the Ride for Roswell and I donate blood to the American Red Cross. One time when I was donating blood, I was put on Channel 4 News. I was telling everybody that was watching that I survived due to blood transfusions.

My mother later told me that it wasn't from blood transfusions that I survived, it was all from healing. Then I told her, "When people donate blood to the Red Cross, they aren't just giving blood. When they donate money for the Ride for Roswell, they aren't just giving money. They are also giving *love!* And that's what helped me survive."

The world is full of good people, if you can't find one, be one!

You are the master of your mind. You are the one who has the power to believe whatever you want to believe. When you focus on aligning your thoughts with action, that is where change happens. Never let anyone belittle your dreams, for only you know how determined you are to accomplish the goals you have set for yourself. Look into your heart and find a reason to make every day special.

Know that you are an amazing, wonderful, complex and beautiful person that deserves true joy. We are all capable of love. Love is the only force capable of transforming enemies into friends and we should share and bare our souls to make the world we live in even more spectacular. Let anger and hatred flow away, let your spirit soar into the universe and be the truly unique person you were born to be. Never be afraid to be who you are. How we overcome the challenges set before us says more about who we are than the mistakes that got us there, to begin with.

Have faith in yourself, listen to your heart and believe that your dreams can come true! Be who you are, be happy, be free, be whatever you want to be. There are miracles around us always. All we have to do is notice them. Stop trying to fit in when you were born to stand out! *Embrace* who you are, *love* yourself and *accept* that you are *amazing* just the way you are. Remeber there's a difference in this world that only you can make because everyone is different in their own way. Life has its ups and downs but you only get one life so do as much as you can, put your heart and soul into everything you do. Love with all of your heart and know that you will get through the bad times because there are always better times ahead -- you just have to believe.

Life is an amazing gift from God that shouldn't be wasted ...

I know that sometimes when you feel down it can be hard to know what your purpose in life is. At times, you may not know where you are going or even how to get to where you want to go. Sometimes life can feel overwhelming and you think it's easier to give in and give up but this is what I have learned, the best way to shift that state is to change that way of thinking to think outside of yourself and realize that whoever you are, whatever you do, whatever you feel your position and status in life is, you can always be an inspiration to someone else.

You can always do something to brighten someone else's day. It may only be a smile or a kind word, but you could change someone's life. You may not even know that you've done it. We all have a past, a history, a wealth of experience and advice that we can often share with other people but forget to take ourselves. We live in a world now where you are never alone. You can connect to people in an instant on the other side of the world if you wish or the best and easiest ones are family and friends.

You are not useless ...

You are not unworthy, but you may have forgotten all the who's and what's you have in life to be grateful for. Perhaps your purpose is to help others before yourself and that will be your way of showing your gratitude. To make a difference in someone's life, you don't have to be brilliant, rich, look beautiful or perfect. You just have to care. You may think your light is small, but it can make a big difference in other people's lives. Let this be a sign that you have a good heart and aren't afraid to let others see it.

Just keep on doing what makes you happy and do it well. Stop worrying about what other people are doing or saying. Follow your heart, trust and believe in yourself and everything will fall into place. The best and most beautiful things in the world cannot be seen or even touched. They must be felt with the heart. One time at the end of a kids baseball game I watched, one of the kids was sad because his team lost. I said, "You will always be a winner as long as you keep practicing and don't give up."

One year my running partner brought his niece to do the Turkey Trot with us. At the end of the run, she said, "It would have been nice if we got an award." I told her, "The big award is in your heart and being thankful that God is letting you do this."

Once when I was back with more disabled people, a person from the People Inc. staff and I heard one of the disabled people say how sad he was about losing a girlfriend. I said, "Everyone we meet in life we meet for a reason. Some come and go so quickly, some stay for years and then leave. It's all part of the way God is giving us the strength to be ready for our future. You have to love and respect yourself."

If you're ever sitting alone somewhere feeling down and sad, remember we all feel like that sometimes. Think of all your blessings and all your gifts in life. Know that you are an amazing and wonderful individual. You have a loving family and great friends who love and care for you very much. Always pray to have eyes that see the best in people, a heart that forgives the worst, a mind that forgets the bad, a soul that never loses faith in God and never stop believing in miracles!

Some of these sayings are already in this book, but I wanted to put them all together so you can read them easier. I have memorized these and often in difficult situations repeat them to myself. That helps me. I hope it will be a help to you as well. I would like to give credit to those that shared these first, I don't know who I just collected them and want to share them with you.

1.   Being rich isn't what you have in your bank account. It's what you have in your heart.

2.   Always pray to have the heart to forgive, eyes that can see the best in everyone, a soul that doesn't ever lose faith in God and a mind that never stops believing in miracles.

3.   Life doesn't have a remote. You have to get up and change it yourself.

4.   If you want to start any kind of physical activity, it always starts with one step.

5.   It doesn't matter how old you are, bullies are always out there. Whenever they say a rude

thing to you, it means that there's something wrong with them, *not* you. Just ignore them and walk away. Keep living your amazing, loving and positive life that God has given you.

6. Sometimes when you are defending yourself, you might also be defending someone that also had gotten hurt in the past by the same person.

7. It's wonderful when you help someone with anything without expecting anything in return.

8. If you keep saying to yourself, "I will change someday," sometimes that someday becomes never.

9. God gave you your amazing life for a wonderful reason, it's your job to find out what that reason is.

10. Nobody's perfect, everybody makes mistakes and needs help sometimes.

11. If you ever find something you can't do, don't let it be in the way of what you can.

12. No matter how hard your life is if you believe that things can get better, they will.

13. Making a hundred friends is not a miracle. The miracle is to make a single friend who will

stand by your side even when hundreds are against you.

14. Let your dreams be bigger than your fears, your actions louder than your words, and your faith stronger than your feelings.

15. Being positive doesn't mean you don't face moments of negativity and doubt. Being positive is consistently and continuously rising above challenges, believing in yourself even when it's hard to and releasing/letting go of any pain. It's about moving forward and getting better.

16. True strength is not what you can do. It's overcoming things you thought you couldn't do. Never let the fear of striking out, stop you from enjoying the game.

17. No matter how good or bad you think life is, wake up each day and be thankful for life. Someone somewhere else is fighting to survive.

18. We don't know what tomorrow will bring. Learn to forgive and love with all your heart. Don't worry about the people that don't like you. Enjoy the ones that love you.

19. Whenever you're trying to help someone, it might seem small to you, but it could feel big to the one you're trying to help.

20.   As you get older, you will start to understand more and more in life, it's not about what you look like or what you own. It's all about the person you've become.

21.   Don't ever change just to impress someone who says you're not good enough. Change because it makes you feel like a better person and leads you to a brighter future.

22.   Nobody's perfect. Everyone makes mistakes. But some mistakes will teach you great lessons & make you a better person.

23.   Sometimes you move on from that person, that job or that situation because you don't want to be unhappy anymore.

The steps in my life so far ...

When I got my first-degree black belt, I started my neighborhood watch job; when I got my second-degree black belt, I began giving speeches; when I got my third-degree black belt, I began writing this book.

I quit Tae-Kwon-Do after ten years. Two weeks later I went back to say thanks to the master. He asked, "Who told you to leave?" My answer was, "God."

I hope you were encouraged by what was written here and that you are blessed by God from some parts of this book. I have learned one thing for certain in my life and that is that God is *awesome*. I wonder what He has for me next ... and for you?

Chapter 10

In Conclusion I would like to Thank a few people...

First my most special thank you!

This is in my heart and I want to share it with you now. My mother is like no other. She gave me life, taught me, dressed me, fought for me, held me, shouted at me and kissed me more than she had to. Most importantly, she loves me and always will. There are not enough words to describe just how important my mother is to me and what a powerful influence she has continued to be. I love you, mom.

There are so many people that I wish to acknowledge. People that encouraged me in my life and because of those encouraging words I was able to do so many amazing things. I have mentioned some of the ones that I want to thank below.

I would also like to personally thank Patty, the friend of my mom's, who ran from the driveway and helped me. She was the first breath of life that I received, she gave breaths to me before the paramedic came and took over. He just happened to show up miraculously .

Thanks to the paramedic that gave me mouth-to-mouth that kept me alive so that I was able to have this wonderful life that I'm having. He had been the car behind the car that struck me and performed the mouth-to-mouth more correctly than Patty had been able to. I would like to thank not only the one that helped me, but also all the paramedics that never get thanked for being there for everybody when they need help.

I would also like to thank People Inc. an agency that without even getting paid took on my case and helped me for a long time before my payments were worked out with the government. They looked at my mom and me and said, "This family needs help and we're going to give it." I have an endless thanks to People Inc. There are so many things that the agency has done with me including helping me write this book. I'll never be able to properly thank them so I would like that to be in this book.

Sue Martin is also someone that was a true friend. She was the one of the staff members at the group homes that I went to. Sue Martin was just a steadfast friend that was always there encouraging with an word for me and not only did she help me but she made me feel important because I was able to share things with her that helped her walk through her life in a more confident way so our relationship was not just one way. I was able to help her get over having lost her husband that had recently passed away. I told her what it was like growing up with an injury and most of all how I had no friends.

I felt the pride of being able to speak life into others as well, which may have been one of the reasons I like speaking in public so much. I like to bring inspiration to others. I like to help others.

I'd also like to thank my grandfather. We really didn't know that much about him, but that we used to look at the picture on the wall. Seeing his uniform was a tremendous inspiration to me even after he died. He always stood for people that would willingly give their lives to help others. I have done a lot of neighborhood watch things on my own. I've been able to help people on my own because of some of the stories that came out of his desire to help people. I attribute that to the inspiration of a grandfather I barely knew.

Friends from the gym Chuck, Mike, Bob and Cindy were coffee buddies of mine. They'd go out for coffee after workingout at the gym. They have Christmas parties together which brings a lot of joy to Jim Pasadeno whom I see a lot because he's a running partner of mine. There is another Jim Roberts that would come to the Christmas party who was my friend too. The one who took care of Christmas parties and had them at his house was Norm Mercedes, a great guy. Sadly he passed away a couple years ago.

There were a lot of great people like Nick Cacciotti and people that have just worked with me through People Inc. that brought a lot of inspiration and, even more so, many opportunities. Nick has a creative mind to think of many different things to do with me. I appreciate Nick's input along with so many others in helping make my life so much fuller and they have my deep and abiding appreciation.

I also have a deep appreciation for the countless workers that work behind the scenes at People Inc. Many I have never met, but they make it possible for there to be a People-Inc. Everybody from Rhonda Frederick, who runs the whole place, down to the people that take care of the office and Megan Logan who does obstacle courses with me and really has brought a lot of joy in providing opportunities for me. Things that would never have been possible if it wasn't for all the people at People Inc. who continue making those opportunities possible. There are so many things that I can do in the Western New York community that really opens up to letting people with special needs get involved.

I also wanted to thank my Tae Kwon Do class and especially my Master who helped me mature through a lot of things that I wouldn't have been able to mature through if it wasn't for him giving me the guidance and confidence. I found out that somebody in a position of authority like that can give you confidence that no one else can give. When another man is willing to take you on and turn you into a man and give you more confidence working with a martial art not only causes you to work in physical areas of your life that are most need of help, it also affects your emotions, your will to do other things you wouldn't do. It also helps in building confidence and all the things that are on the inside even though it seems like all your working on these things on the outside like your muscles but how much more it does on the inside to who you are as a person and that helps you to become a man.

From Ryan's Helper With This Book

I met Ryan as I helped him write this book. The more I got to know him, the more inspired I became with his life's story. To have survived the physical and emotional trauma he has and to have accomplished all that he has is remarkable.

As I listened to his story, I detected no pride in his accounts of the various trials he faced and was able to overcome. He accomplished one goal after another. He gave all thanks, gratitude and glory to God, his mother and the friends he made along his incredible journey. His lack of pride also showed when he readily accepted suggestions I made as we pieced this book together.

To work alongside someone whose life is dedicated to serving God and helping people was a pleasure and an honor. I'm certain that you will find this book more than a story about Ryan, but will refer to certain parts of it over and over. It has many insightful and inspiring parts that you will reread often.

Sincerely,

Leo Ward

A short note from my Mom

I'm Ryan's mom and I have been asked to add some input here about my side of this story. And maybe say something to other's that find themselves a parent in a situation similar to mine.

I will not lie, this was the hardest thing I have ever been through, I was a single parent and had another son, Steven plus a fulltime job. It is an on going trial to this day but he is my living miracle.

The biggest thing I will tell you is to have patience, the healing takes a very long time and there will be days when you are angry, confused, tired and depressed. Please remember your child is having these feelings too. Praise the small milestones. It will encourage them to go on.

Get some knowledge about brain injury (or whatever your situation might be). I read a lot of books, articles and talked to a lot of people. Every brain injury and recovery is different. Do not expect the same outcome as someone else.

Be prepared to fight for your child's rights. I took on school systems, teachers, lawyers and even other people. Remember people are afraid of what they don't understand.

Find some support groups and agencies if you can. We lived in a small town and this wasn't available to me. I truly believe it would have been helpful to have those.

If you have other children remember, they need you too, especially if they are young. They don't understand the depth of this.

Finally be sure to take some time for yourself. If someone you trust volunteers to stay with them for a while ACCEPT IT. You need time for yourself. My heart goes out to those of you reading this book and are dealing with this type of injury. Its a very long road to travel with a lot of good and bad. Stay strong and never be afraid to ask for help.

www.ingramcontent.com/pod-product-compliance
Lightning Source LLC
LaVergne TN
LVHW021611080426
835510LV00019B/2511